"The Colours of My Life" - The Artwork of Cher-Antoinette, Barbadian Emerging Artist

THE ARTIST

Barbadian Forensic Scientist, Visual Artist & Writer, Cher-Antoinette is multi-faceted and commenced her artistic journey in earnest in 2014 where she decided to let her work speak to her life. The journey was further enhanced by the many challenges faced as a single parent raising two boys, the insecurity that is seeded by societal expectations and the strength it takes to continue to be honest with oneself.

A self-taught artist, her process involved finding what media she was most comfortable with and this resulted in works of Watercolour, Pen & Ink, Charcoal, Alcohol Inks and Oil Pastels. She has been successful at the island's National Independence Festival of Creative Arts (NIFCA) in Photography 2009, Literary Arts 2011/2012 and Fine Arts 2012/2013. She has published a poetic anthology MY SOUL CRIES in 2013, VIRTUALIS: A New Age Love Story in 2014 and ARCHITECTS OF DESTINY: Poetry & Prose in 2015.

Cher-Antoinette's style is varied and has been said to be quite unique.

"At the beginning I tried to emulate or even imitate what some of my mentors were producing, especially in relation to Barbadiana. After a while I realized that being an artist was speaking your truth and having the words translate to images on your canvas, or for me more my acetates. My work highlights the Synergy of Life and Art."

An emerging artist, Cher has gotten much attention since the launch of **C-Toi Wearable Art**, a jewelry line that showcases her acrylic fluid art. Each piece is one-of-a-kind and brings art to the average person in an affordable format. The pieces are also enhanced with healing crystals such as amethyst, hematite and black onyx.

Cher-Antoinette's Home Studio was opened in August 2017 and is located three minutes' drive from the Airport.

Cher-Antoinette's Studio
#35 Hopefield, Christ Church
Barbados BB17084
cherantoinettestudio@gmail.com
www.cherantoinettestudio.com
246-2398617

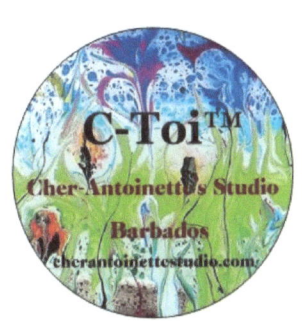

"The Colours of My Life" - The Artwork of Cher-Antoinette, Barbadian Emerging Artist

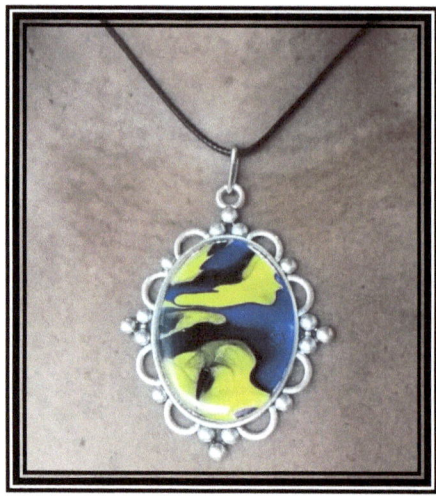

C-Toi Wearable Art is created by the artist Cher-Antoinette. Her Acrylic Fluid Art is gaining much attention but understandably the cost of canvases may be prohibitive to some.

"My art brings me joy and I want everyone to know that art is for everyone and everyone deserves to own art. With that in mind, I found a way that my images or part thereof can be enjoyed and at a price point affordable to most. It is hoped that eventually persons can own the larger fine art pieces. I am grateful."

The Independence Collection will be on display at the exhibition.

Cher-Antoinette is the embodiment of a Renaissance Woman. One of the Caribbean's leading forensic scientists; she is also a mother of two, an award winning, published writer, and a talented visual artist. Now add designer to the list with the recent launch of her *C-Toi* line of *Wearable Art*.

As a visual artist, Cher-Antoinette's singular explorations emerged to flowing expressions of time and space with her critically acclaimed one-person exhibition, March 2017, at the EBCCI Gallery, UWI-Cave Hill, Barbados. The series of paintings and objects which comprised the exhibition *"Just Call Me Sarah"* were a remarkable statement from an artist who has arrived.

Fully in control of her media and technique, Cher-Antoinette has provided another visual treat, with vivid scenes of the Barbadian landscape as well as a series of color-drenched, expressive, sensual paintings, which make a statement all on their own. We are honored to present *"The Colours of My Life"* featuring the art and artistry of Cher-Antoinette in celebration of Barbados' 52nd Anniversary of Independence, November 30, 2018.

Anderson M. Pilgrim
Diaspora Now Inc.

My Colours

My Life

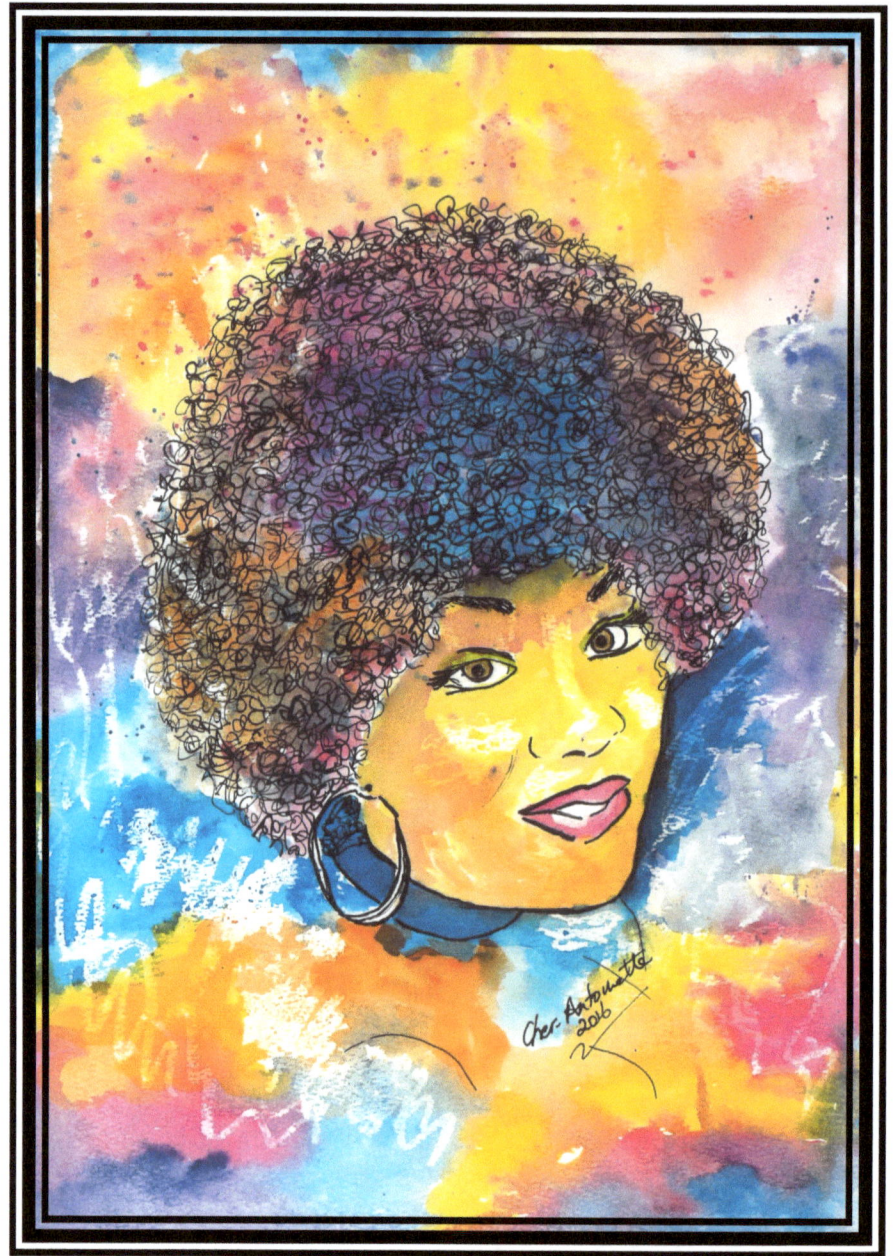

"The Colours of My Life"

Pen & Ink/Watercolour on Paper

11"x14" matted 16"x20" in frame

US $680.00

Item #1

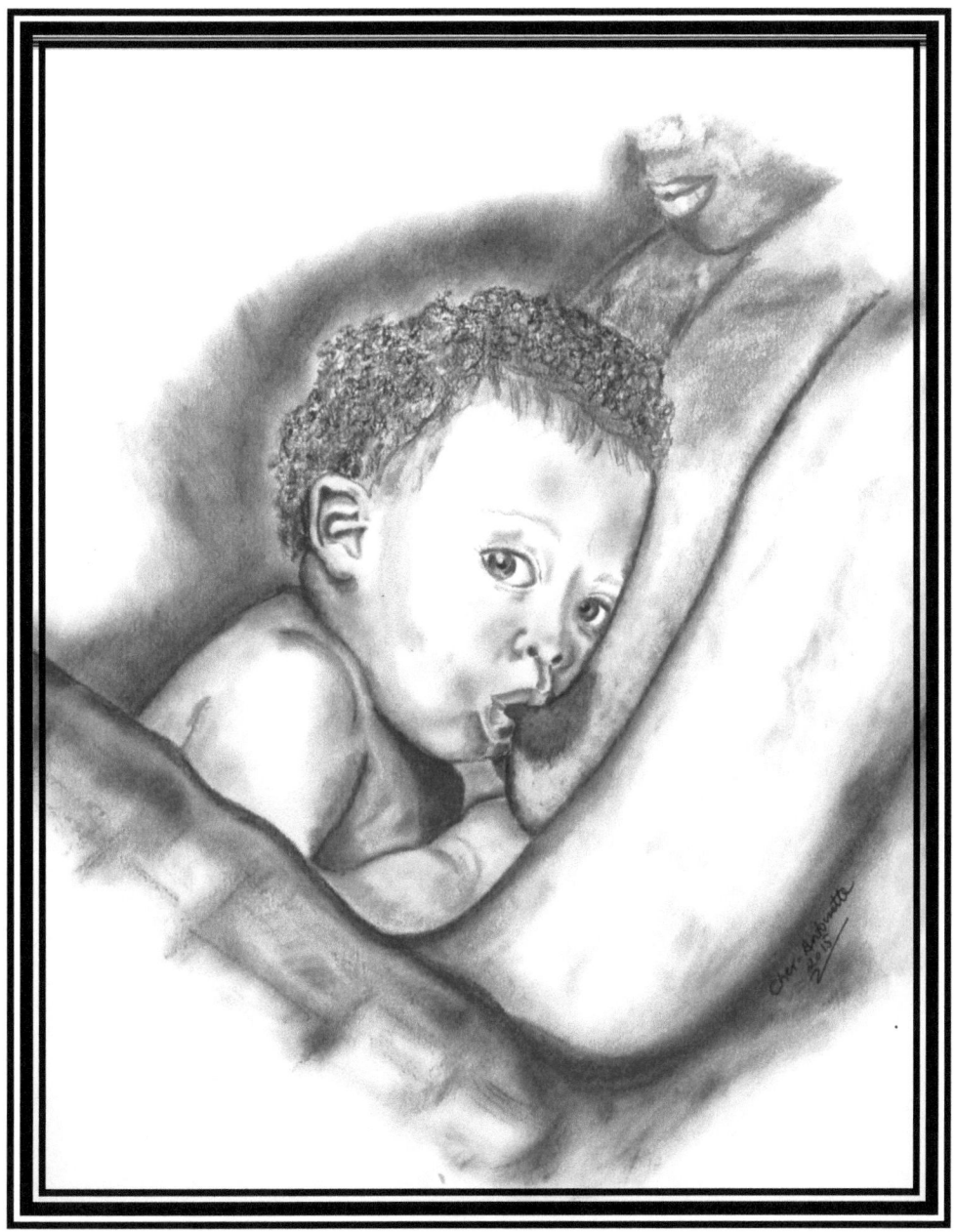

"Contented"

Charcoal & Graphite on Paper

11"x14" matted to 16"x20" in frame

US $680.00

Item #2

"The Colours of My Life" - The Artwork of Cher-Antoinette, Barbadian Emerging Artist

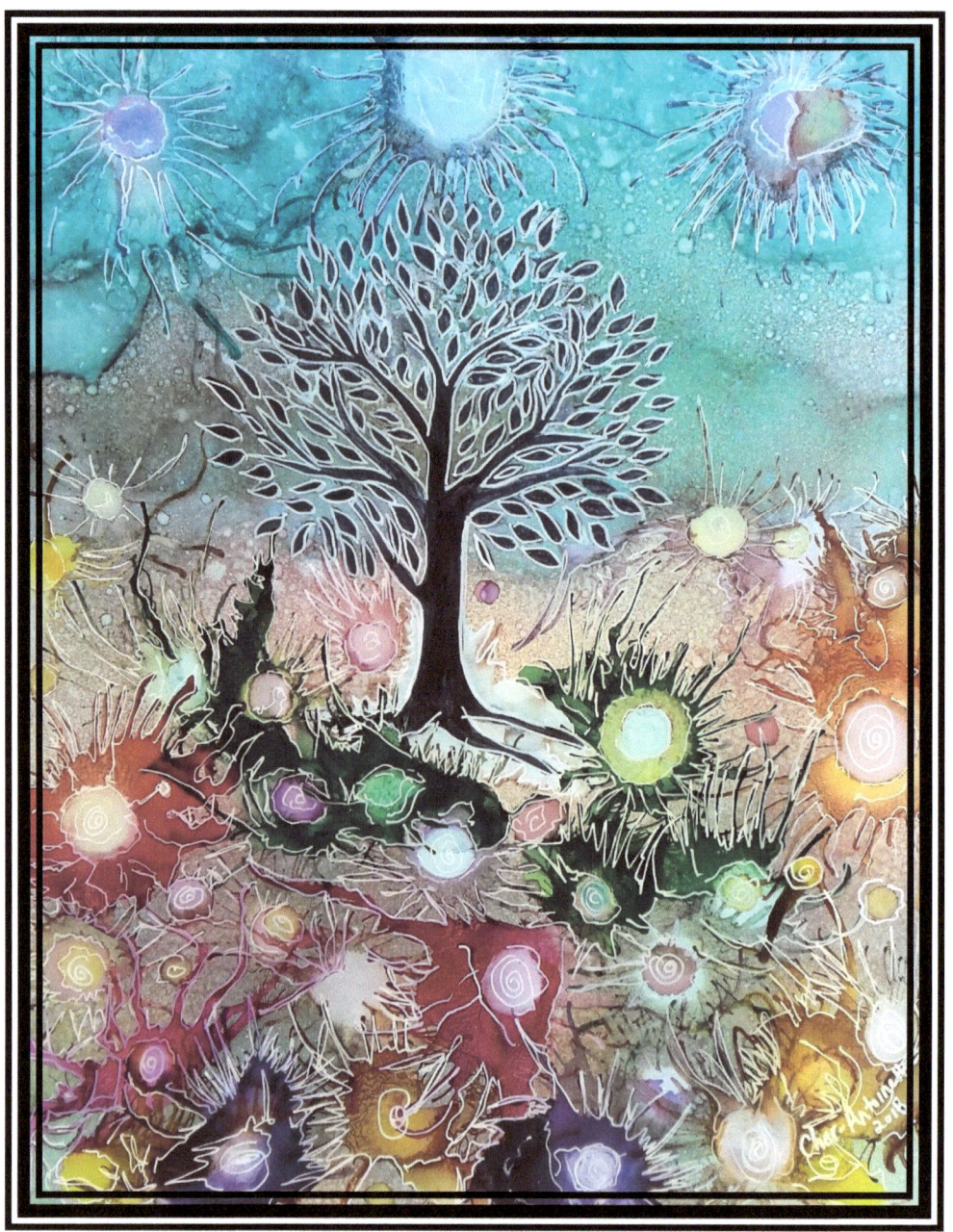

"Celebration"

Alcohol Inks on Yupo

11"x14" matted to 16"x20" in frame

US $680.00

Item #3

"The Colours of My Life" - The Artwork of Cher-Antoinette, Barbadian Emerging Artist

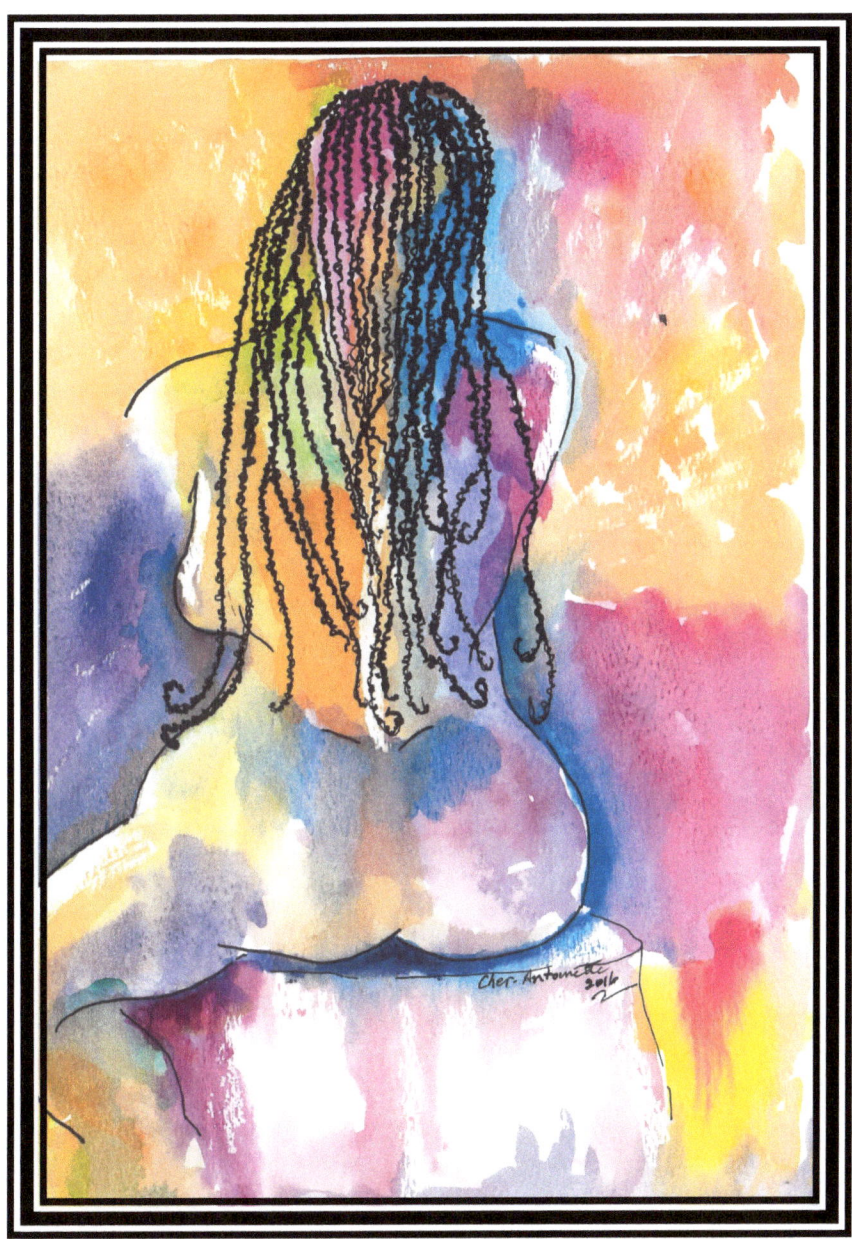

"I Am Enough!"

Pen & Ink/Watercolour

8"x10" matted to 11"x14" in frame

US $450.00

Item #4

"The Colours of My Life" - The Artwork of Cher-Antoinette, Barbadian Emerging Artist

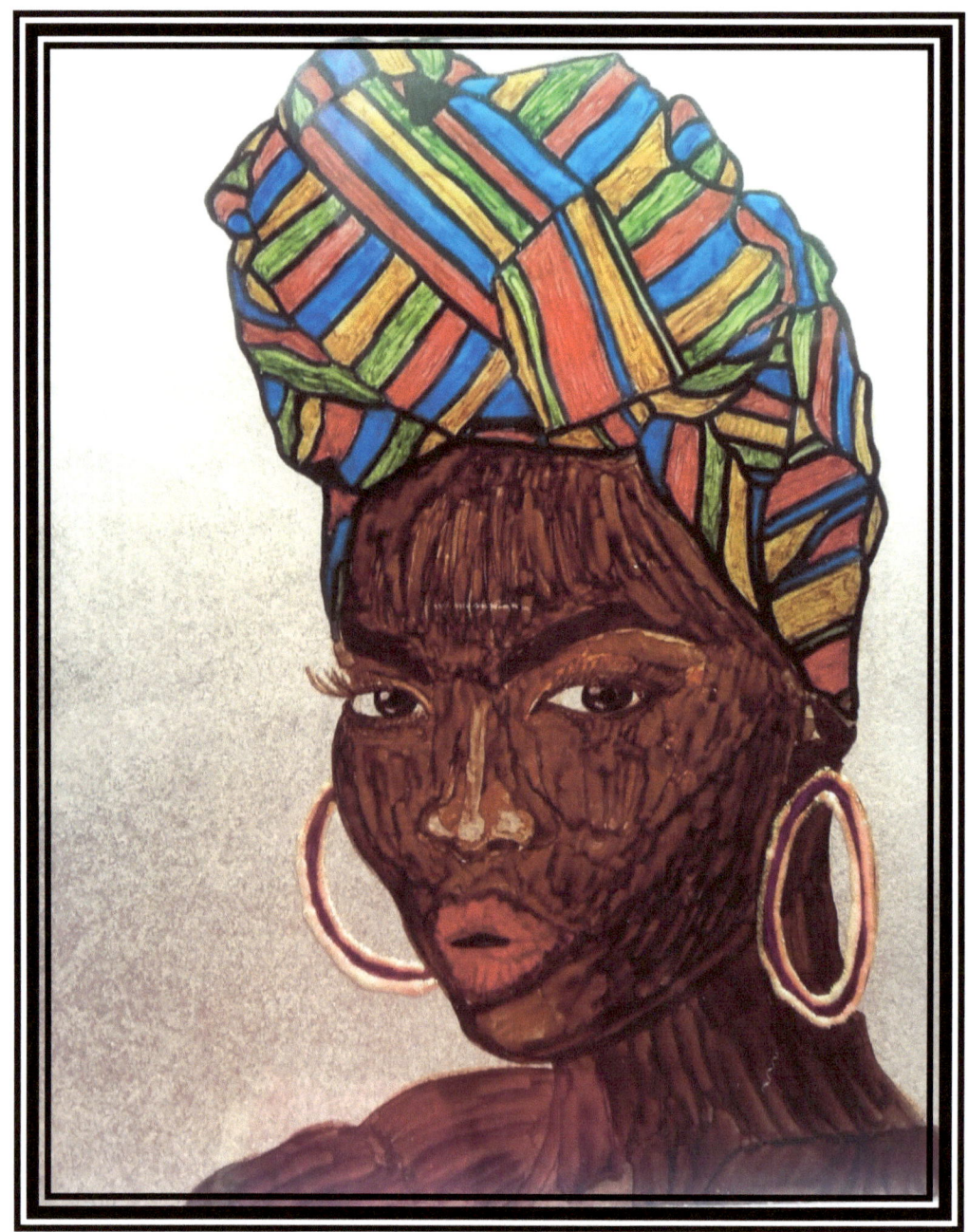

"Mahogany Gold"

Alcohol Inks on Acetate

11"x14" matted to 16"x20" in frame

US $850.00

Item #5

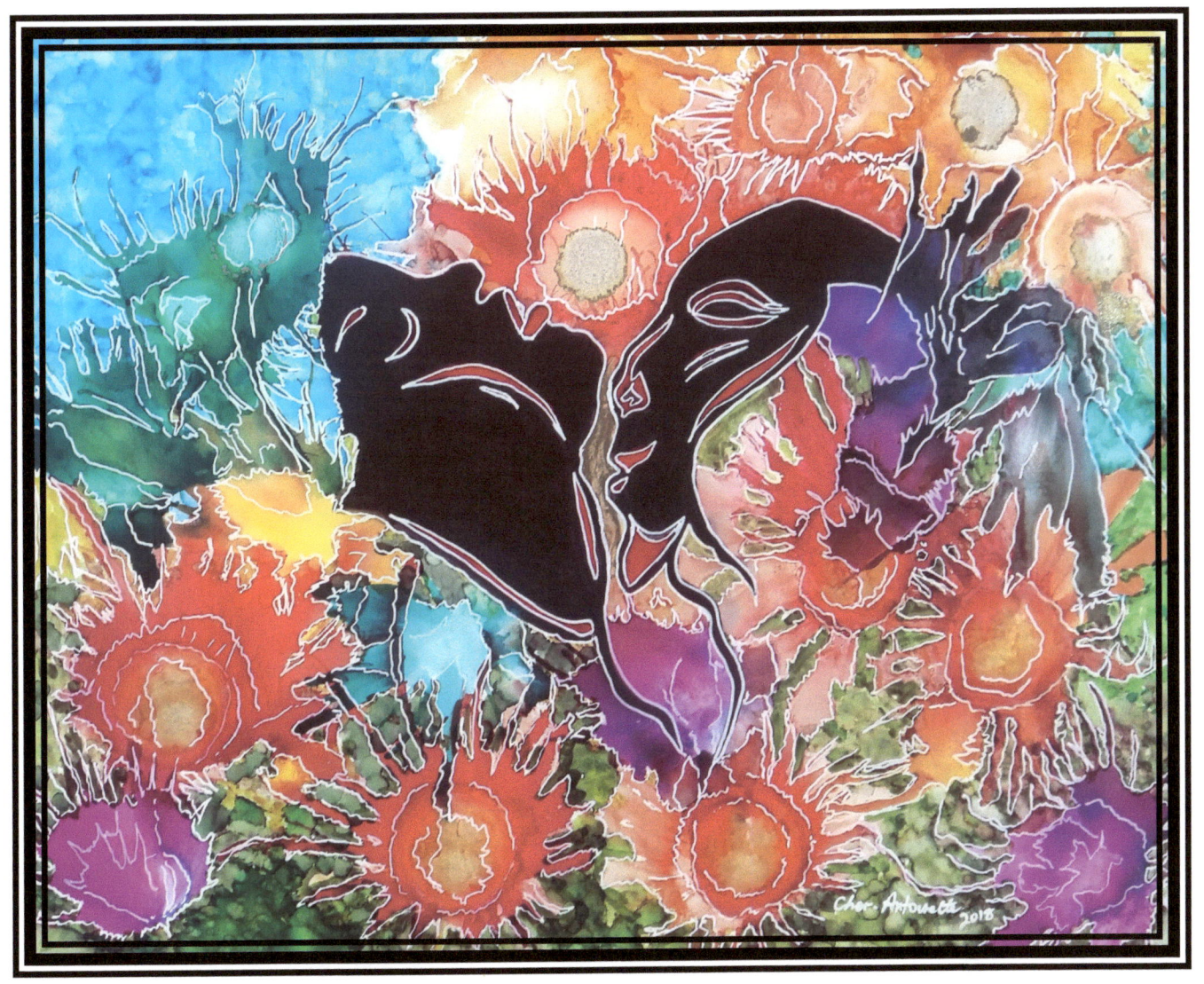

"Passion"

Alcohol Inks on Yupo

11"x14" matted to 16"x20" in frame

US $680.00

Item #6

"The Colours of My Life" - The Artwork of Cher-Antoinette, Barbadian Emerging Artist

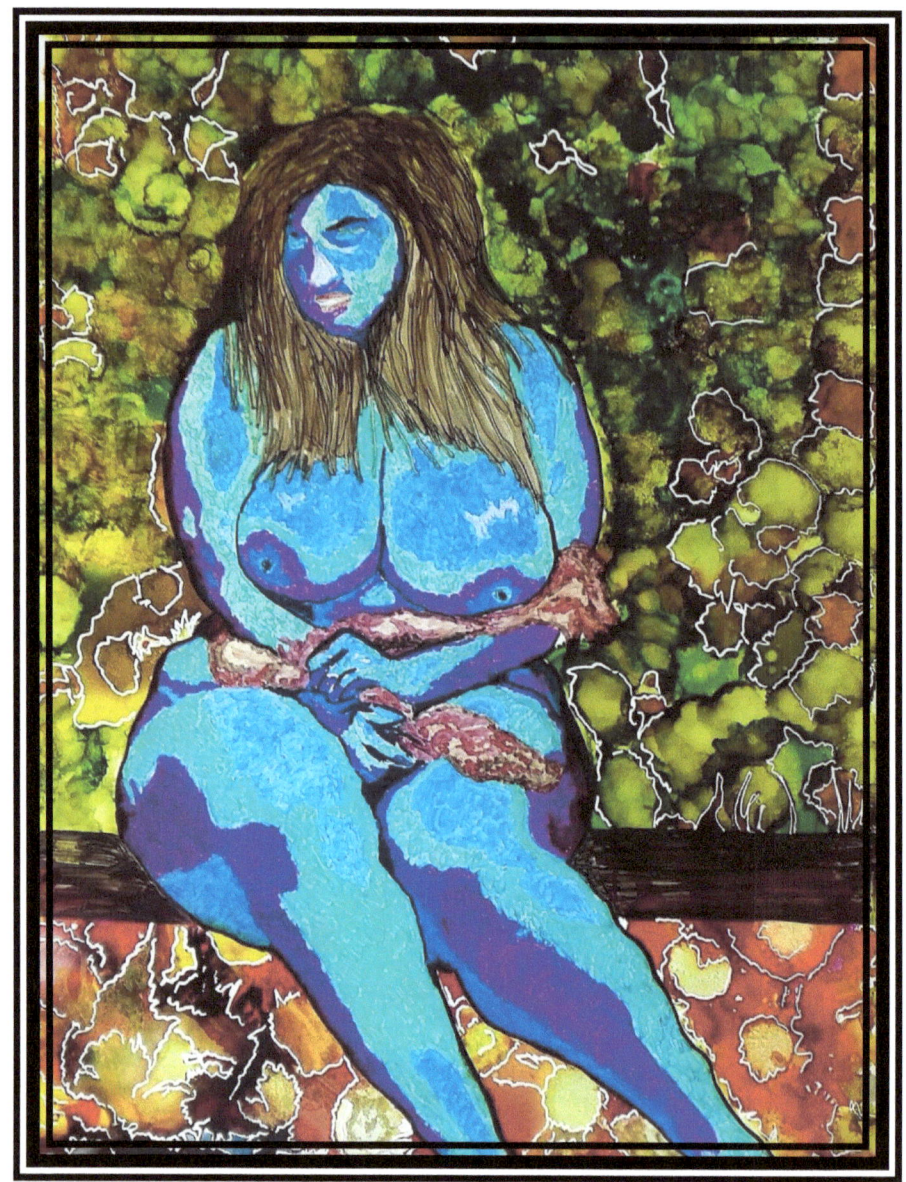

"Reflective Blues"

Alcohol Inks on Acetate

11"x14" matted to 16"x20" in frame

SOLD

Item #7

Barbadiana

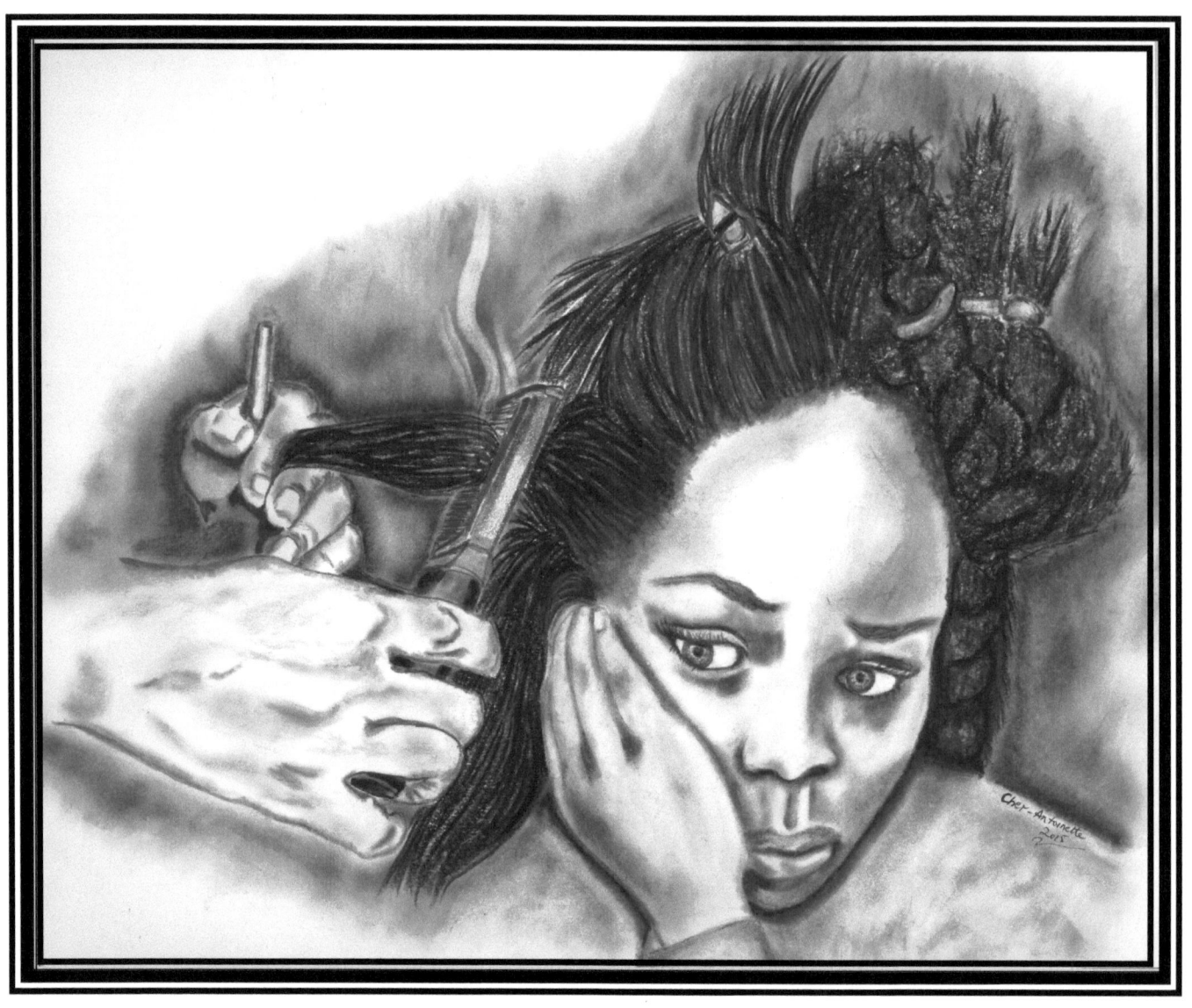

"Look, I'm A Big Girl Now!"

Charcoal & Graphite on Paper

11"x14" matted to 16"x20" in frame

NFS

Item #8

"The Colours of My Life" - The Artwork of Cher-Antoinette, Barbadian Emerging Artist

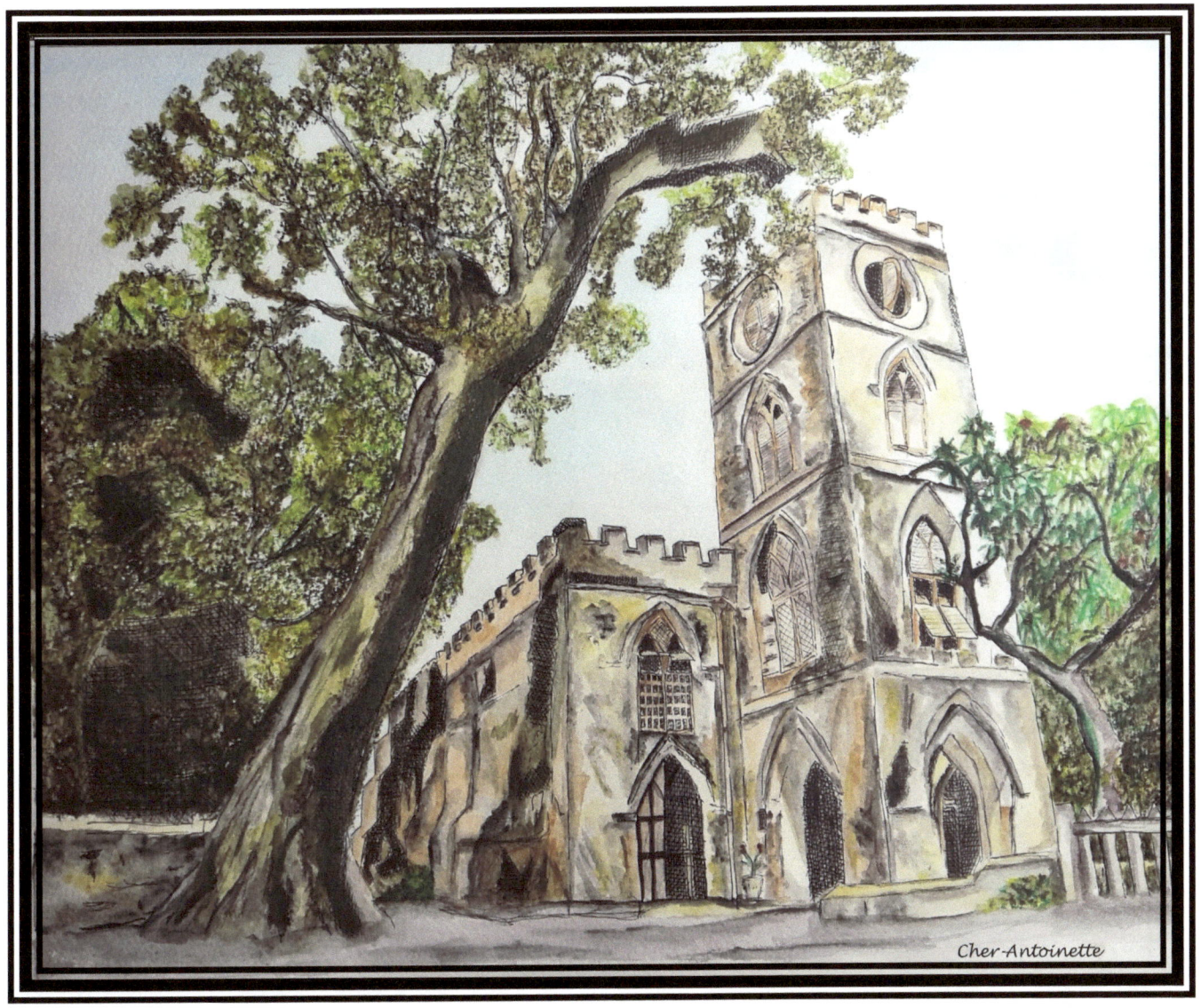

"St. John's Parish Church"

Pen & Ink/Watercolour on Paper

11"x14" matted to 16"x20" in frame

US $750.00

Item #9

"The Colours of My Life" - *The Artwork of Cher-Antoinette, Barbadian Emerging Artist*

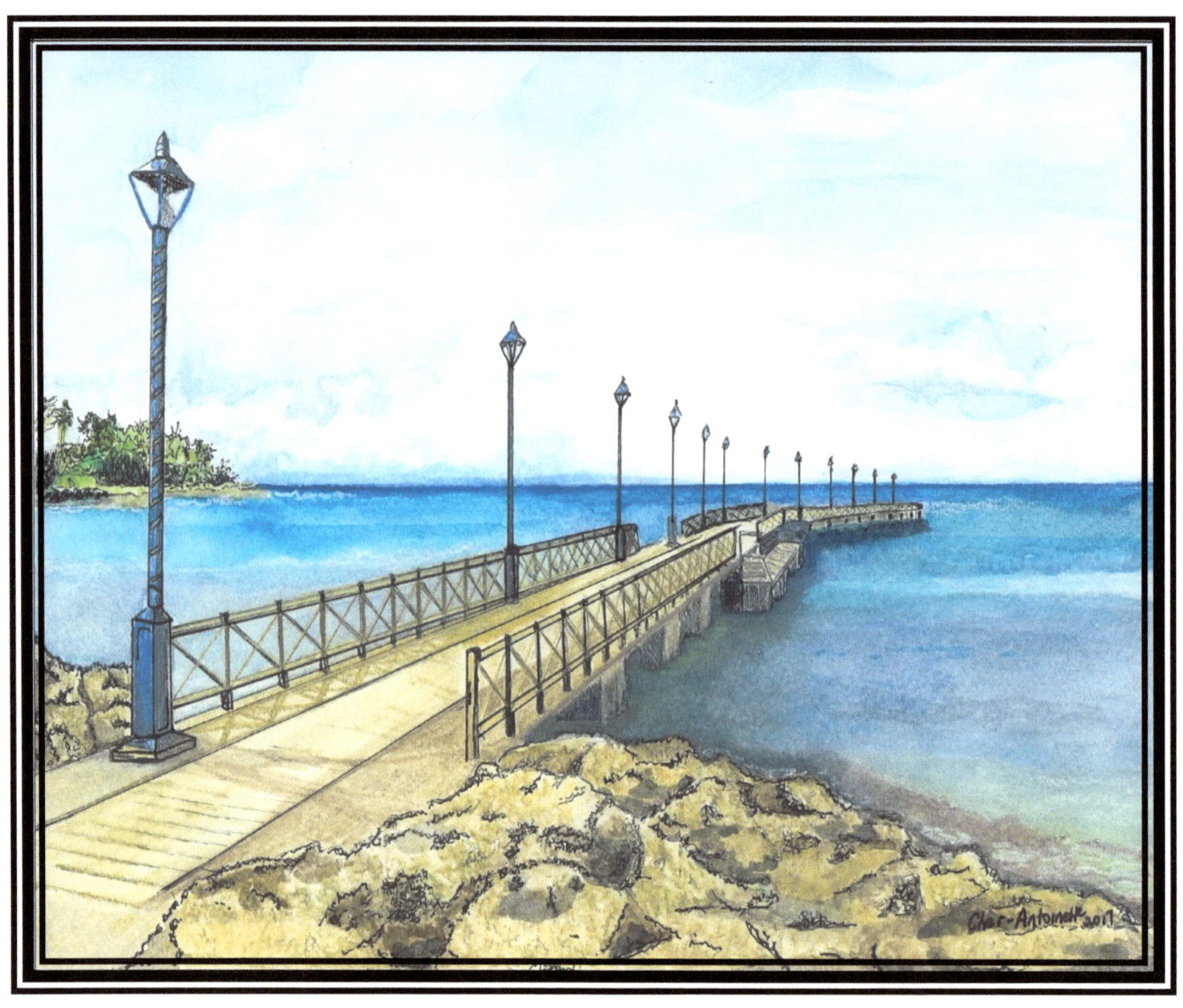

"Speightstown Jetty"

Pen & Ink/Watercolour on Paper

8"x10" matted to 11"x14" in frame

US $480.00

Item #10

"The Colours of My Life" - The Artwork of Cher-Antoinette, Barbadian Emerging Artist

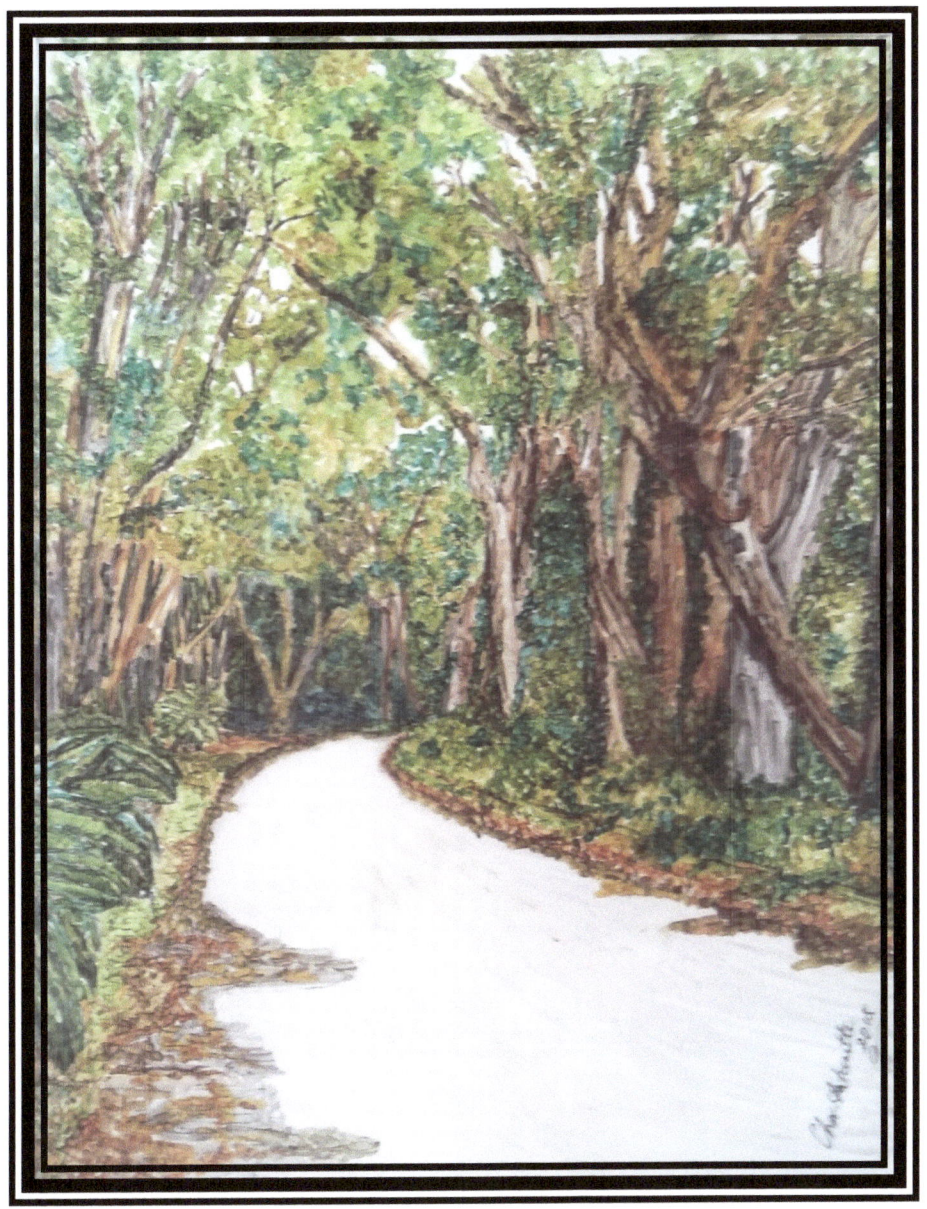

"The Grove at Cherry Tree Hill"

Alcohol Inks on Acetate

11"x14" matted to 16"x20" in frame

US $800.00

Item #11

"The Colours of My Life" - *The Artwork of Cher-Antoinette, Barbadian Emerging Artist*

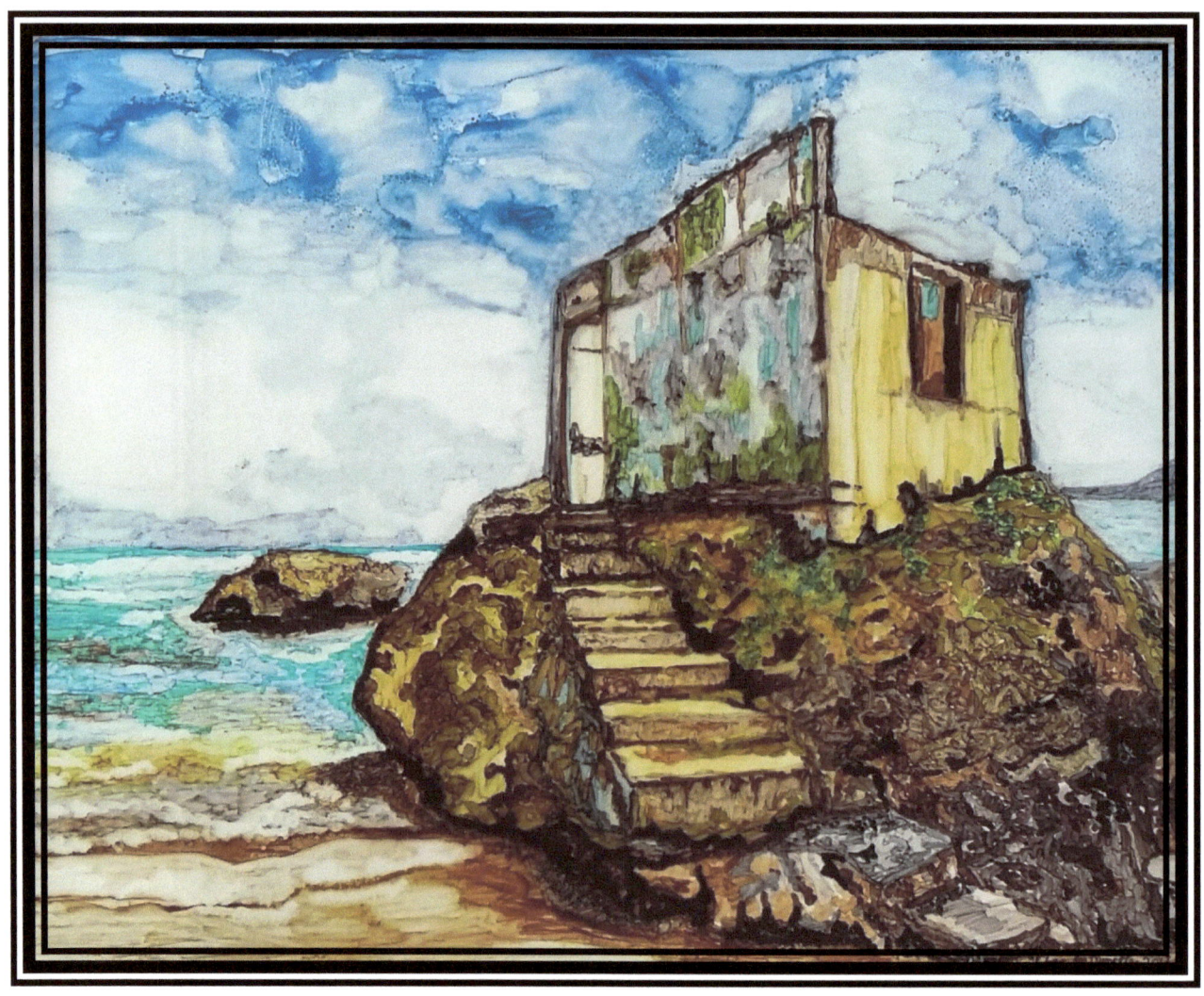

"The Old Bath House at Bathsheba"

Alcohol Inks on Acetate

11"x14" matted to 16"x20" in frame

US $850.00

Item #12

Madonna

"The Colours of My Life" - The Artwork of Cher-Antoinette, Barbadian Emerging Artist

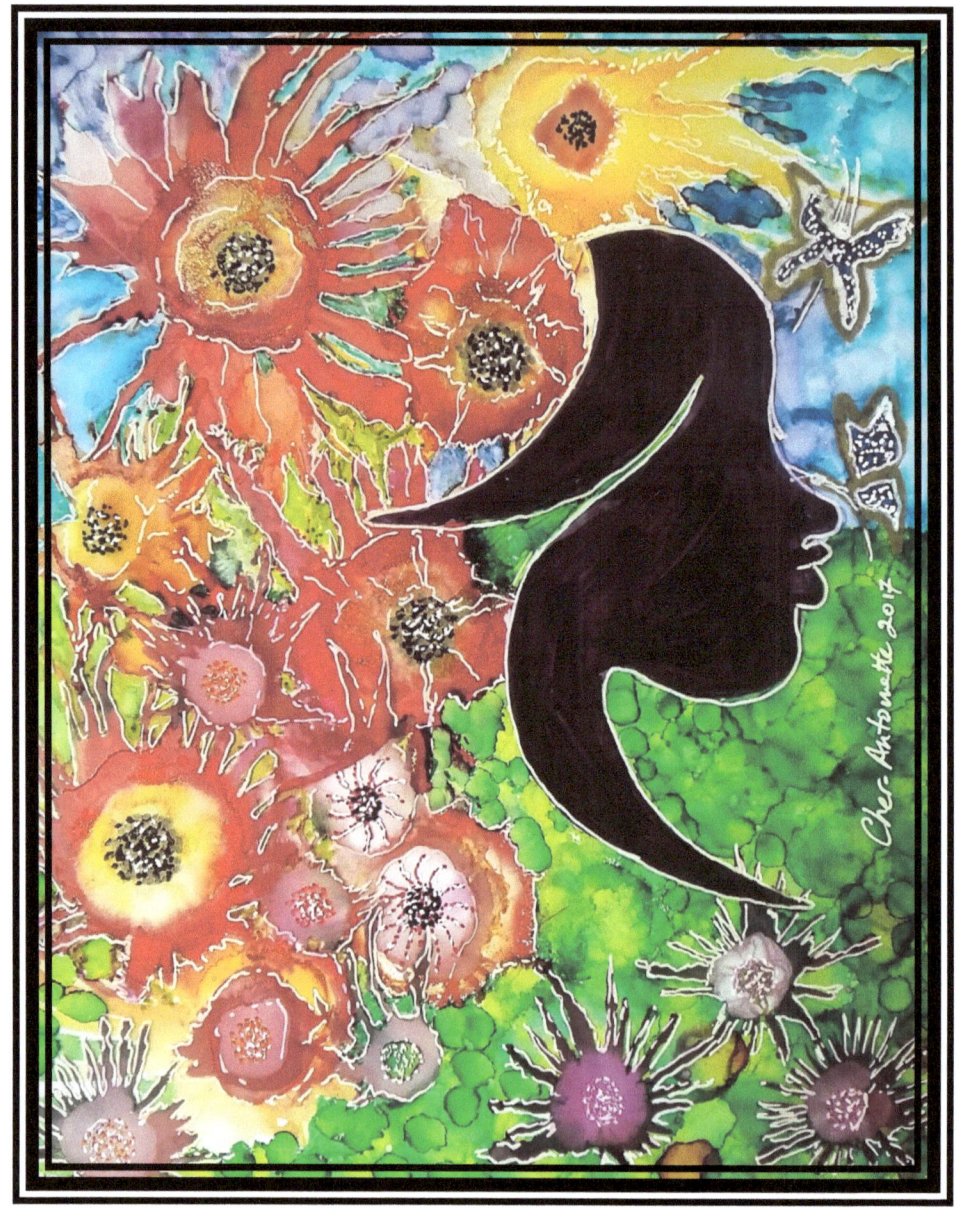

"Beauty Within"

Alcohol Inks on Acetate

8"x10" matted to 11"x14" in frame

US $450.00

Item #13

"The Colours of My Life" - *The Artwork of Cher-Antoinette, Barbadian Emerging Artist*

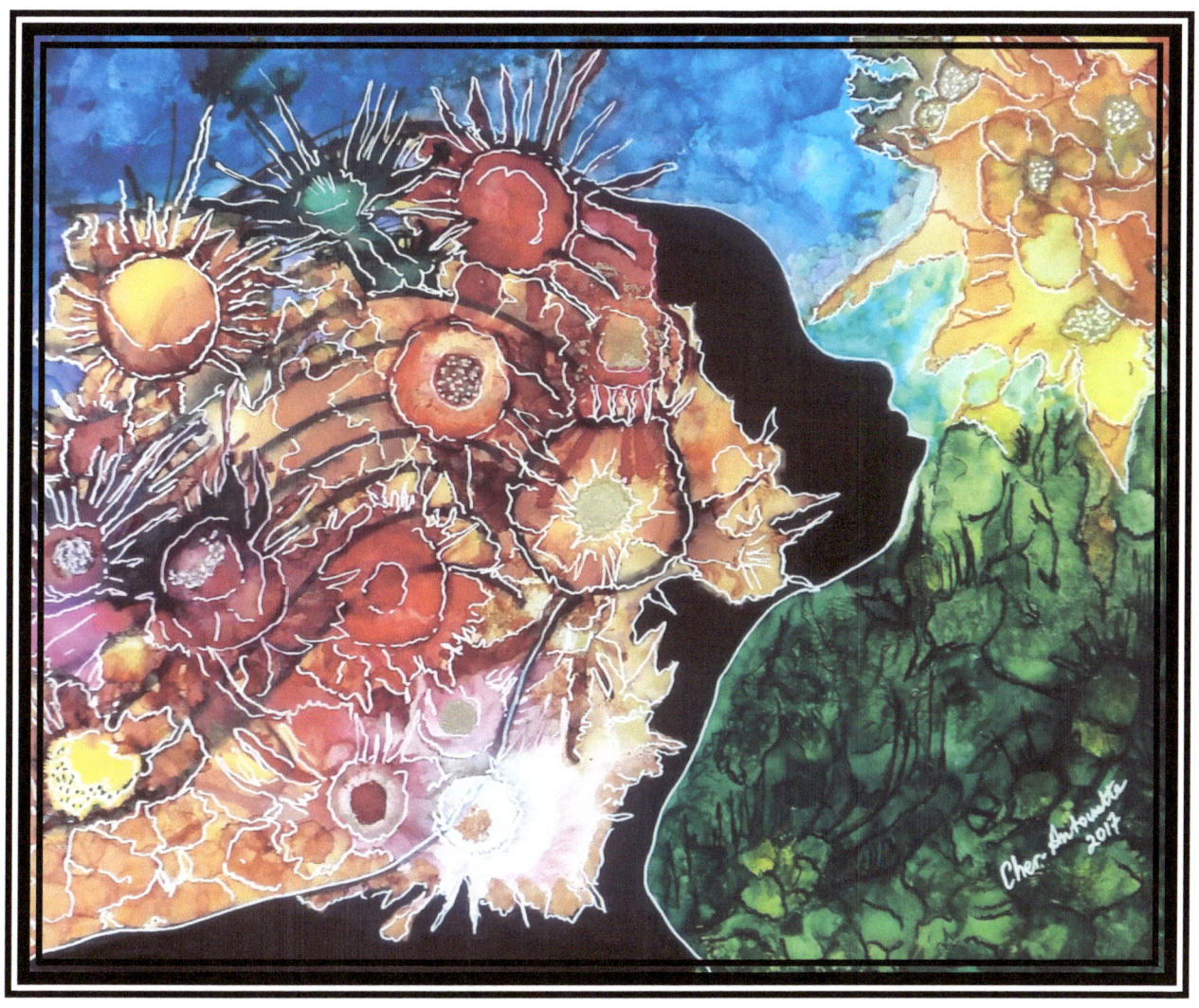

"Rejuvenation"

Alcohol Inks on Yupo

11"x14" matted to 16"x20" in frame

US $700.00

Item #14

"The Colours of My Life" - The Artwork of Cher-Antoinette, Barbadian Emerging Artist

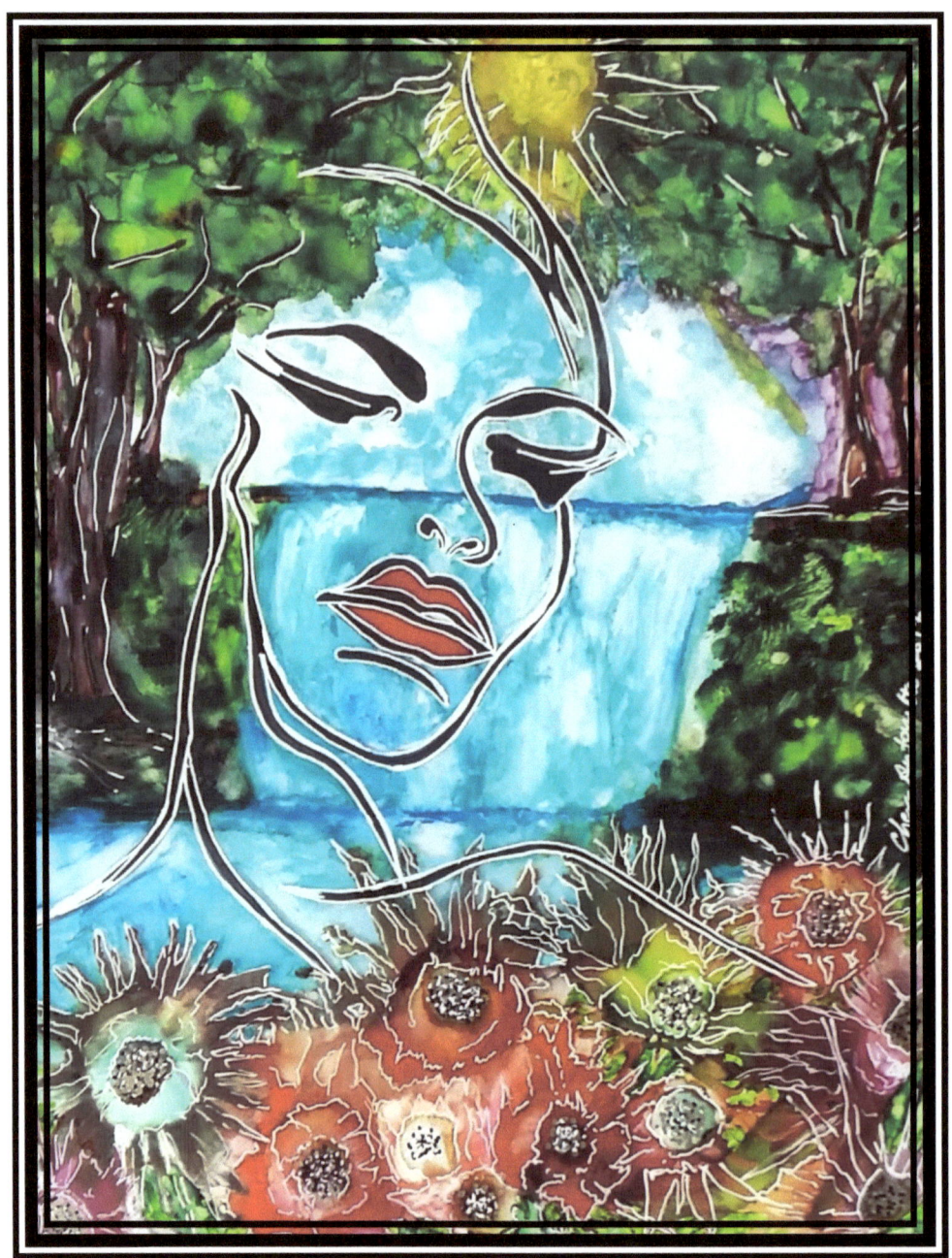

"Healing"

Alcohol Inks on Acetate

11"x14" matted to 16"x20" in frame

US $700.00

Item #15

"The Colours of My Life" - The Artwork of Cher-Antoinette, Barbadian Emerging Artist

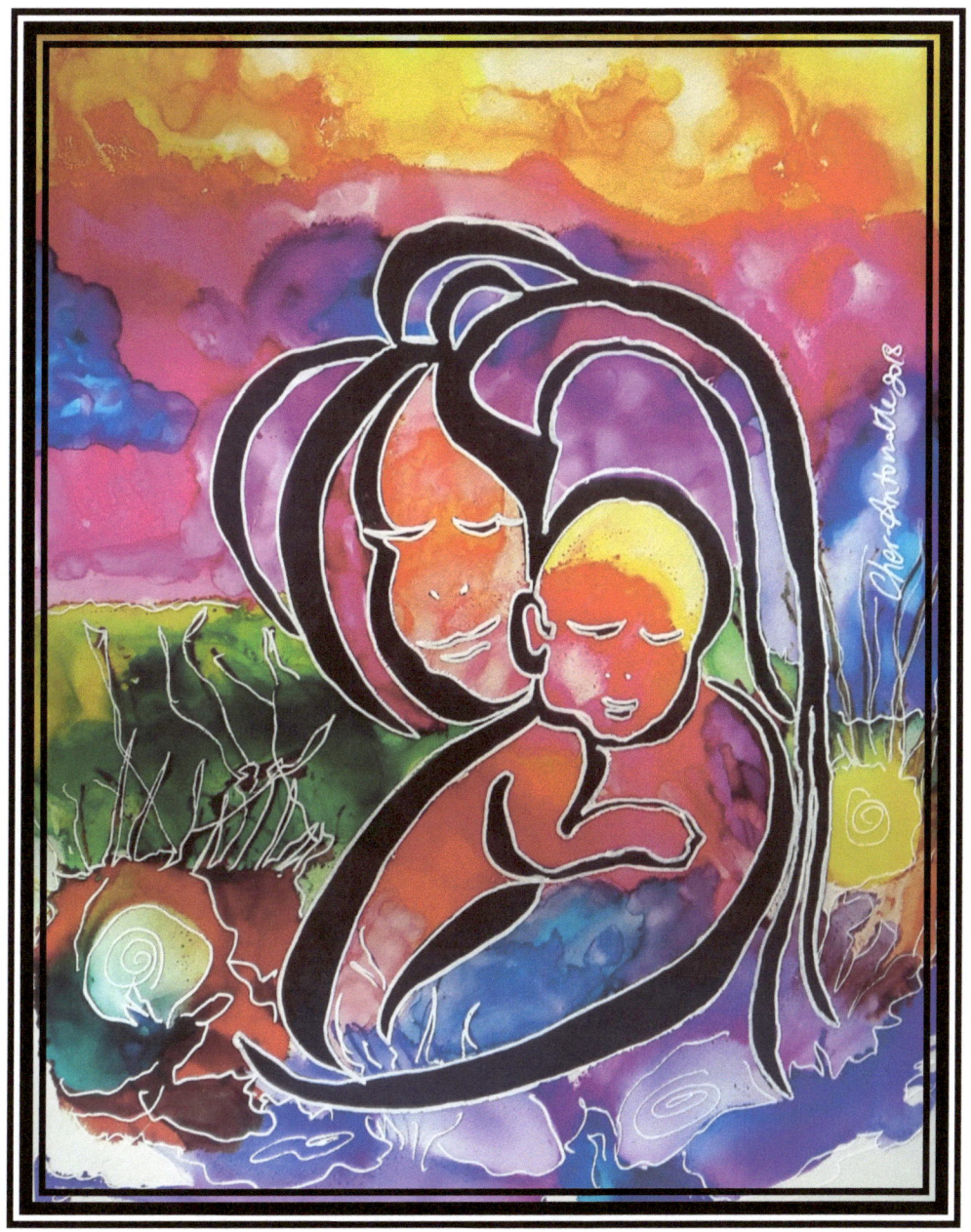

"Hush"

Alcohol Inks on Acetate

8"x10" matted to 11"x14" in frame

US $450.00

Item #16

"The Colours of My Life" - The Artwork of Cher-Antoinette, Barbadian Emerging Artist

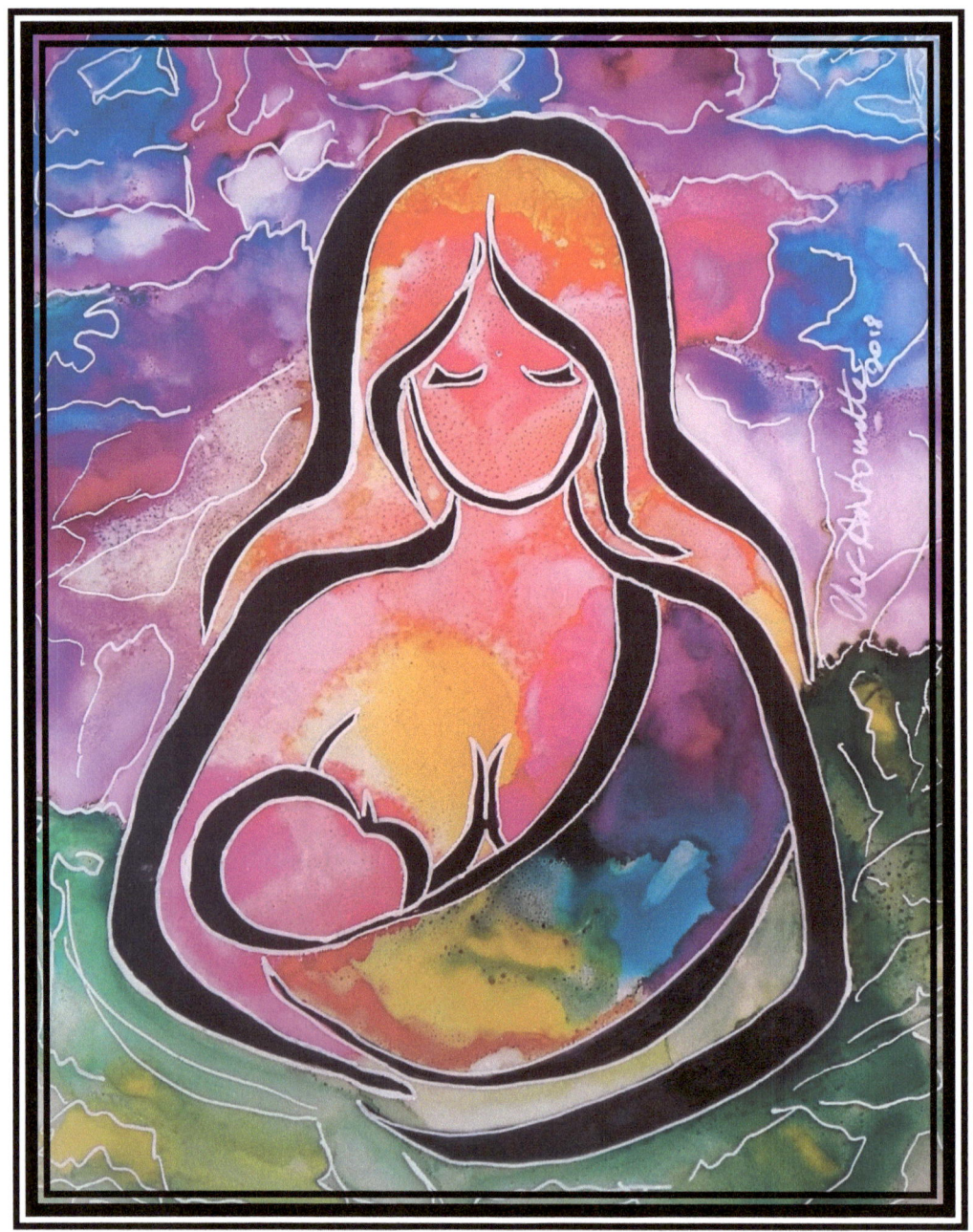

"Bliss"

Alcohol Inks on Acetate

8"x10" matted to 11"x14" in frame

US $450.00

Item #17

"The Colours of My Life" - The Artwork of Cher-Antoinette, Barbadian Emerging Artist

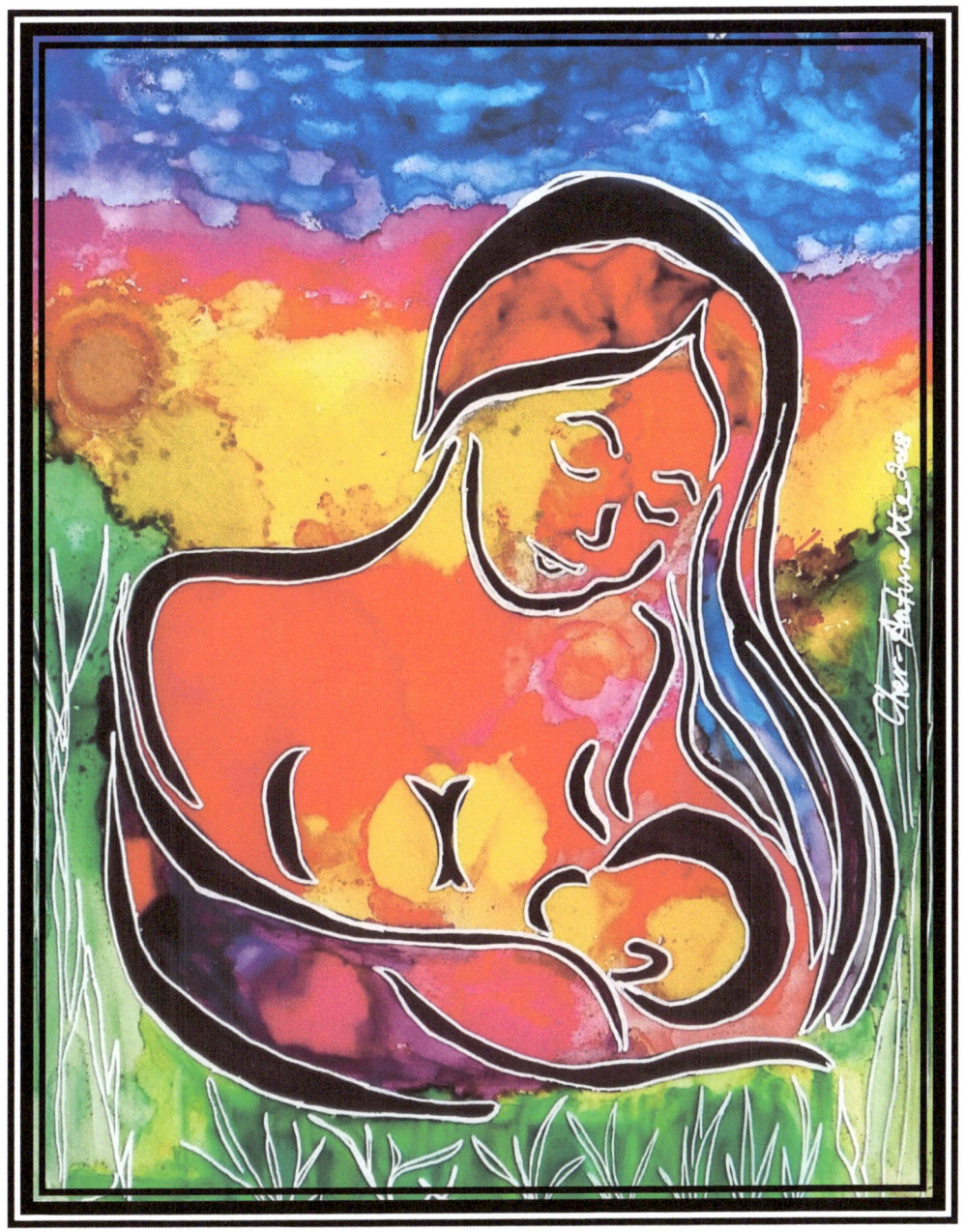

"Of Nature Born"

Alcohol Inks on Acetate

8"x10" matted to 11"x14" in frame

US $450.00

Item #18

LIMITED EDITION PRINTS

Limited Edition Prints are available for the MADONNA SERIES only. There will be a print run of 25 and all prints are 8"x10" matted to 11"x14" and will be signed, numbered and dated.

The L.E. Prints :	Rejuvenation	**Cost: US$100**
	Healing	
	Beauty Within	
	Hush	
	Bliss	
Open Edition:	Look, I'm A Big Girl Now!	**Cost: US$50**
	Contented	
	I Am Enough	
	Speightstown Jetty	
	St. John's Parish Church	

Contact Information:

    Diaspora Now Inc. : ampilgrim@hotmail.com - (646)267-8831

    The Embassy : washingtoninfo@foreign.gov.bb - (202)939-9200

    The Artist: cherantoinettestudio@gmail.com - (246)239-8617

Payment Information:

All major credit cards accepted as well as Pay Pal and Venmo.

Checks payable to Diaspora Now Inc.

Payment plans are available for original artwork only.

Thank You

I wish to express my appreciation to all of you who have taken the time to come out to see the work at my studio, exhibitions or who have displayed genuine interest in any of my projects.

To my family, friends and supporters, your being on this journey with me fills me with such blessings and gratitude - I am empowered.

Cher-Antoinette

Artwork in this catalog is NOT to be reproduced or changed without the written expressed permission of the artist.

www.ingramcontent.com/pod-product-compliance
Lightning Source LLC
Chambersburg PA
CBHW051838210526
45473CB00005B/1931